The Canine Cure: A Guide to Breaking Your Dog's Bad Habits

Jessica M. Broyles

ACKNOWLEDGMENTS

First, I'd like to acknowledge my husband, George, who is always supportive of all of my endeavors. Also, I'd like to thank Merrilie Hindsley who patiently edits all of my writing and also her husband, Daniel Hindsley for all his expertise in photographic and graphic arts. Finally, I'd like to acknowledge Pixabay and Adobe for the use of their free stock photos taken by their very talented photographers.

Table of Contents

Introduction

So, you brought home a new addition to your family or you have a dog that has picked up some undesirable habits. Either way, it is never too soon or too late to give your furry friend some better habits while dropping any unwanted ones.

Welcome to the world of dog training! If you're reading this book, chances are you're looking for ways to break those bad habits and help your dog become a well-behaved companion. Don't worry, you're not alone. Many dog owners find themselves in the same boat and struggle with similar issues. But the good news is that with patience, consistency, and the right training techniques, you can help your dog overcome their questionable manners and live a happy, harmonious life with you.

This book provides a comprehensive guide to breaking your dog's questionable manners, using positive reinforcement and science-based training methods. I believe that all dogs are capable of learning and changing their actions, and I'm here to show you how to make that happen. Whether you're dealing with barking, jumping, chewing, or any other problematic behavior, I've got you covered.

These and other common behavior problems can drive even the most caring pet lover a little crazy. I will give you insights and the tools necessary to help your dog learn better habits. My straightforward advice and step-by-step instructions will help to eliminate your pup's misbehavior for the long term.

We'll start by discussing the importance of knowing your dog. Then, understanding your dog's behavior and body language, so you can identify the root cause of their misbehavior. We'll delve into the various training techniques and methods you can use to help your dog overcome these issues. From clicker training to shaping and differential reinforcement, to even ignoring your pet, you'll learn about the most effective ways to communicate with your dog and teach them new, desirable manners.

Throughout the book, you'll find practical tips and real-life examples to help you put the training techniques into action. Some of the most common naughty behaviors to the more unhealthy or even dangerous pet actions will be discussed. From simple chewing to aggressive actions. These tried-and-true remedies, if done properly will last a lifetime.

I'll also discuss common pitfalls and how to avoid them, so you can stay on track and achieve your goals. Whether you're a seasoned dog owner or a beginner, this book is designed to be accessible and easy to follow.

You may be wondering what your canine companion is thinking. Is there something going on in his or her mind while they lay there and watch you go about your daily routine? I can tell you; they are busy studying YOU 101. They want to know everything there is to know about you. Why?

It's because dogs love unconditionally. That's why they're called man's best friend. Like in the song by Linda Ronstadt, they are hopelessly devoted to you. When you take on the responsibility to have a dog it's with the promise that it will be for life. This book will give you the tools needed to keep this promise.

So, let's get started on your journey to establishing good behaviors or breaking your dog's bad habits and building a stronger bond with your furry companion. With patience, consistency, and a positive approach, you'll be amazed at the changes you can make in your dog's demeanor and your life together. Happy training!

Chapter One

Know Your Dog

Body Language

Reading your dog's body language is essential to understanding and communicating with your pup. Every dog has their own personality and unique set of behaviors, so it's important to get to know your dog and learn what their body language means.

To begin, understand that dogs communicate primarily with body language. It is their primary form of communication, and it's important to be able to read it correctly in order to interact successfully with them.

When your dog is feeling untroubled and comfortable, they will often have a calm posture. This includes a neutral head position, loose body, and a relaxed tail. They may also appear to be in a playful mood, with a wagging tail. A posture that appears unruffled can indicate that your pup is feeling content.

A tense posture can mean that your pup is feeling anxious or scared. If they seem nervous or stiff, it may indicate that he or she is feeling aggressive or ready to react. Their head may be down and their tail tucked between their legs. They could also be panting heavily or they could be yawning, and their body may be rigid.

If your dog is feeling aggressive, his or her body language will be more assertive. Their tail may be up and their ears in a forward position or flattened back. They may also be barking or growling. This may also indicate that he or she is ready to react.

A key body language to look for is facial expressions. Dogs have a wide range of facial cues that can tell us a lot about what they're feeling. A relaxed expression can indicate that your pup is feeling comfortable and content, while a tense one can mean that he or she is feeling anxious or scared. When your dog raises his or her inner eyebrow muscles, this produces the telltale mournful, soulful look you know all too well. The one that makes you willingly give your pup anything she wants, even if it is off-limits.

Your dog's tail position will also divulge a lot about how he or she is feeling. A tail that's hanging low can indicate that your pup is feeling relaxed. A high tail or a tail that is tucked between their legs can indicate that your dog is feeling anxious or scared.

Pay attention to your dog's ears. When a dog is feeling content, their ears will usually be in a neutral position, pointing down. When a dog is feeling alert or aggressive, their ears may be pointing up or back.

Notice your dog's eyes. If they are wide open and focused on something, it can indicate that your pup is feeling alert or excited. When he is feeling tense, his eyes may appear rounder than normal or they may show a lot of white around the outside. This is sometimes called "whale eye." Dilated pupils can also be a sign of fear or arousal. If your dog's eyes appear glassy, he may be feeling threatened, stressed, or frightened.

If your pup's eyes are half-closed or unfocused, it can indicate that they are feeling calm and even serene. Think back to the last time your dog made eye contact with you. Did you get the feeling that he or she meant to do this and perhaps was even trying to convey a message? For example, you throw your dog's favorite toy, and it lands behind the couch. Your dog can't get to it even though he really wants to. What does he do? He looks at you for help. What do you do? You help him by retrieving the toy, of course.

Pay attention to the context in which your pup is displaying certain body language. For example, if your pup is exhibiting a tense posture and wide eyes in the presence of another dog, it may indicate that they feel threatened or scared. If they are exhibiting the same body language when you come home, it may indicate that they are excited to see you.

A new environment or the presence of other animals can influence your pup's body language. Your canine companion's emotional state can change quickly. By being aware of your dog's unique reactions to new situations, you can get a better understanding of how they are feeling and what he or she may be trying to communicate.

Interpreting Sounds

Interpreting the sounds your dog makes is an important part of understanding what's going on in their mind. Every dog has its own unique set of vocalizations that can help us understand what they're trying to communicate.

Barking is one of the most common vocalizations that dogs use. The type of bark, its intensity, and the accompanying body language can all tell us a lot about what your pup is trying to say.

A single, low bark may indicate an alert or warning to another dog, while a series of high-pitched, excited barks may mean your pup is excited to see you. A series of loud barks directed at you can mean your pup is trying to tell you something. For example, they may need your help to retrieve a toy or maybe they want to be let in or out.

Whining is another vocalization that can tell us a lot about how your pup is feeling. A low, soft whine can indicate that your pup is feeling anxious or scared, while a high-pitched, excited whine may mean that your furry friend is feeling happy and playful.

A low, rumbling growl may indicate that your pup is feeling threatened or aggressive, while a high-pitched growl may indicate a play growl.

Your pooch may also use a variety of other vocalizations such as yelps, howls, and whimpers to communicate. A yelp can indicate surprise or pain, while a howl can mean that your pup is feeling lonely or anxious. Whimpers are usually used to express distress or fear, and can be a sign that they are feeling overwhelmed or scared.

No matter which vocalization your pup is using, remember they are just trying to communicate with you. Pay attention to the sounds he or she makes, and understand what each sound means. Doing this can help you better understand your pup and build a stronger bond with them.

Understanding Your Dog's Breed

When it comes to training your dog, it's essential to understand their breed and their inherent traits. Every breed of dog has its own unique personality, instincts, and tendencies, and these factors can play a significant role in shaping their behavior. By understanding your dog's bloodline, you can tailor your training techniques to their individual needs.

If you have a high-energy breed like a Border Collie or Australian Shepherd, you'll want to provide plenty of physical and mental stimulation to keep them happy and well-behaved. If your pup has a more relaxed bloodline like a Basset Hound or a Bulldog, you'll need to be patient and gentle, as these dogs are more sensitive to stress and negative reinforcement.

Understand your dog's breed history and the roles for which they were originally bred. Herding dogs were bred to control and direct livestock, so they tend to be highly intelligent and eager to please. Hunting dogs were bred to track and pursue game, so they are more independent and driven by their instincts. By understanding these traits, you will get a better sense of what motivates your dog and what kind of training techniques to use.

Consider your dog's individual personality and background. Dogs are unique creatures, and their experiences and environment can shape their behavior just as much as their breed. A dog that has been mistreated or neglected in the past may have trust issues and may be harder to train than a dog with a stable and loving background. They may flinch at human contact or be overly submissive or even aggressive.

What Does Your Dog Like?

So, how can you get to know your dog's specific bloodline as well as their personality? You can start by talking to your vet or a local dog trainer who can give you an overview of your dog's breed traits and tendencies. You can also keep a journal noting your dog's specific actions. For example, you'll want to note their likes and dislikes, habits, and tendencies. This information will help you create a customized training plan that considers your dog's individual needs and preferences.

Spend time getting to know your dog. Before you start a training program, test them on which treats they like best. Just like humans, our pups have their own unique likes and dislikes. Your fur baby needs to feel that what you're offering is worth it. Whether it's ham, chicken, cheese, or peanut butter. Do they prefer hard treats to soft ones? Are they partial to cracker or cookie type snacks or do they like the meatier ones?

When choosing toys, don't pick the ones according to your own preferences in colors and materials. Find out what your pup likes. It may look cool in the store, but if your dog doesn't like it, it may go untouched. Your dog may even shy away from it. Does he or she like rubber toys, plastic toys, or furry toys? Do they like hard, soft, big, or small? Some dogs appreciate an empty plastic bottle more than an expensive toy from the pet store.

Some dogs love to be touched by you while others tend to prefer it less so. They may even become distressed if you become too loving. Notice your dog's reactions and see if he or she finds tactile interactions rewarding.

Chapter Two

What You Need to Know About Training

Know the Basics

The first step is to understand the basics. Before you can start teaching your dog more advanced commands, it is important to understand the basics of dog training. Here are a few things you should know.

- Timing: When training your dog, timing is everything. If you are too late to reward for good behavior or too early to scold them for bad conduct, it won't be effective. Enough can't be said about a teachable moment. If you find your dog doing what you want them

to do, even by accident, be sure to reward them for it. For example
if you're trying to teach them not to pick up something you've
dropped and they refrain from picking it up because they were
engaged in something else, show them the dropped item and
reward them for not picking it up.

- Positive Reinforcement: Positive reinforcement is a key part of
training your dog. You should always reward them with praise,
verbal acknowledgement, or treats when they do something right. I
refer to this technique a lot because of its importance to training
your pup.

- Consistency: Consistency is key. If you don't stick to the same
commands, rules, and rewards, your dog won't be able to learn
effectively. Everyone in the household should be giving the same
commands and following the same rules to keep it consistent for
your pet.

- Patience: Training takes time and patience. Don't expect your
canine companion to learn everything right away. It takes
repetition and consistency to get the desired results. As you know,
all dogs are different and come to learning with their own set of
tools. Whether it be their breed, prior learning, age, etc.

Establishing Leadership

Establishing leadership when training your pup is an important part of
ensuring that he or she understands boundaries and behaves appropriately.

Establish a clear hierarchy in which you are the leader and your pup is the follower.

The Essentials

- The first step is to make sure that you are always in control. This means that you should be the one to initiate all interactions, including feeding, playing, and walks. This will help them understand that you are the leader, and they should look to you for guidance.
- Establish clear rules and boundaries for your dog. This can include not allowing them to jump on people, having them stay in their designated area at certain times, and if you so choose, not allowing them on the furniture.
- Be consistent with your rules and make sure that your pup understands that they must adhere to them.
- Be calm and assertive when training them. Speak in a firm, authoritative voice and make sure that he or she understands what you expect of them. Do not yell or use physical punishment, as this can lead to confusion and fear in your pup.
- Reward them when they are behaving appropriately. This will reinforce the desired actions and help them understand what is expected. Positive reinforcement is the best way to ensure that your pup is learning and following the rules.

Leadership training should be fun for you and your dog. If your pup is feeling stressed or overwhelmed, take a break and try again later. This training should be tailored to your pet's individual needs and personality. Every dog is different, so take the time to get to know them and understand what works best for him or her.

Remember, this training is not about being harsh or punishing your dog. It's about teaching them what's appropriate and rewarding them for following the rules. Be patient and understanding, and realize that it takes time for them to learn and understand. This is not a one-time process, but rather an ongoing method that requires patience and consistency. Be sure to review the rules and boundaries regularly, and continue to reinforce the desired conduct with rewards.

Nothing in Life is Free (NILIF)

For dogs with behavior issues, trainers often use programs such as NILIF which works along the principal that the dog must do something to earn what he or she wants. This is effective because the dog is issued a structured set of rules that are consistently reinforced. The dog learns what he or she needs to do in order to get the things it wants such as food, petting, playtime, treats, etc. Dogs can't tell us what they need through speech so oftentimes behavior problems and anxiety are the result. These poor animals are left to fend for themselves in deciding how to live in our world without guidance that makes sense to them.

Dominance Myths

The myths in dominance theory, such as not allowing your pet to sleep on the bed, eat first, go through doorways first, or walk ahead of you have no bearing on whether your dog will look to you for guidance. The rules of your relationship are up to you.

The training techniques I offer teach owners to positively and gently influence their pups to act in a manner that befits a loving, positive relationship. Most dogs and their owners have wonderful, mutually-rewarding relationships, even if the dog is allowed to sleep on the bed, eat alongside their human, and walk in front of them on a leash.

Chapter Three

Identifying and Understanding Bad Habits

When it comes to breaking your dog's bad habits, the first step is to identify and understand them. Misbehaviors can range from chewing on furniture to barking excessively, and can be caused by a variety of factors.

In order to identify and understand your dog's discipline issues, it's important to observe them closely. Dogs tend to repeat behaviors they find rewarding, but some of these are the same bad habits we humans want them to break. The key to stopping them is to make it more rewarding to not repeat them.

Keep a Log

Keep a detailed log of your dog's conduct. This can include information such as specific actions, the time of day, and in what locations the observations occur. It can also include your dog's body language and energy level before and during the behavior.

Note what environment and surroundings any misdeeds occur in and if there have been any recent changes to the environment and/or surroundings. Try to determine what triggers the misconduct. This will help you to identify which environment, routine, or situation may be the cause of the problem.

The Three Ws

Consider the context in which these behaviors occur. Such as when they happen, where they happen and with whom they happen. If you can answer these three things, you will begin to understand what's going on with your dog and you will be able to form some conclusions.

Underlying Causes

These new (or old) questionable habits may be due to one or more things, but before you can find a cure, you need to understand the cause. We'll touch more on this in the next chapter but for now, some of the most common causes are: boredom, lack of exercise, separation anxiety, and fear.

Please note: Some bad habits, such as destructive chewing or excessive barking, may be due to a medical condition or a symptom of hyper-stress and anxiety. In these cases, consult with a veterinarian to rule out any underlying health problems before addressing the issue.

Making a Difference

Understanding the root causes of your dog's discipline issues is key to changing them to something more acceptable for you both. This might include changing the environment, providing more exercise or mental stimulation, providing positive reinforcement, or some other form of management. Dogs are individuals and what works for one dog may not work for another. Always consider the dog's breed, age, and personality. Some breeds are predisposed to certain behaviors, such as herding or digging, and this should be considered when addressing the misconduct. Puppies and young dogs may not have fully developed impulse control, and older dogs may have physical or cognitive limitations that affect their behavior.

Training is Key

Teaching your dog the basic commands of obedience training like 'sit, come, and down' may not seem related to a barking, chewing, or jumping problem, but these commands help you to manage your pup when misbehavior occurs. Better management means they can be easily controlled and become a part of the family and go to events, instead of uncontrollable, misbehaving and having to be left at home or shut away from the party by themselves. Some things as simple as your dog greeting someone politely, coming back when they are called or walking safely and controllable on a leash are basic desirable behaviors you want to see in your pet.

A well-trained dog, under supervision, is safer to have around family and friends, and is at a lower risk to themselves than an uncontrolled dog. Remember, at the end of the day, dogs are dogs and can sometimes be unpredictable. A dog that comes back when called, in the face of dangerous situations, (example: where they could get hit by a car) has an obviously positive impact on his or her own welfare.

Sometimes we as pet parents send the wrong signals to our canine companions. For example, if your dog is growling or barking at another dog, you may try to pick them up or pet them. If you do this, your dog will think it's okay and even desirable to act aggressively because you rewarded them for it.

The same goes for whining, barking, and howling to get your attention. If you react to this sudden change in dog behavior and start talking to your dog, playing with them, or giving them snacks, the behavior will continue.

Some dog behaviors are instinctive, some are bad habits formed over time, and some could be signs of an underlying health condition.

Instinctive behaviors include digging, chewing, chasing, and rolling in dirt or poop. They make sense to your dog and are even enjoyable, much to your chagrin. You can train your dog to minimize or stop these habits, but it won't be easy.

Bad habits like resource guarding, jumping on people, climbing on furniture, begging for food, clingy behavior, etc., are encouraged by our behavior toward our dogs. To stop these types of habits you will need to set clear boundaries and be consistent. Be sure to provide your pooch with comfort, safety, and enough food so they do not have to claim these things for themselves.

Excessive licking, eating poop, defecating, and urinating indoors along with growling or biting can be due to a health condition. If these are occurring, have your veterinarian give your pup a check to determine if there is something going on medically.

Ultimately, by understanding your dog's naughtiness in detail, you will be able to develop a customized training plan that addresses the specific issues, and help your dog learn new, more desirable manners.

Chapter Four

The Root Cause of Unwanted Behaviors

Bad habits happen to us all, including our pets. Your dog may not be biting his nails or staring at a phone for too long before bedtime, but it's possible they have picked up some poor habits throughout their lifetime, whether you've had them since puppyhood or adopted them at an older age. Your canine buddy is a special part of your family, and you want to ensure they are well-behaved, happy, and healthy.

Unfortunately, sometimes your dog may display problematic behaviors that are hard to handle. To effectively break these bad habits, it's essential to understand the root causes. Let's explore some common causes of troublesome misdeeds and provide examples to help you identify them.

Common Causes

Boredom: Dogs are active and curious creatures that need mental and physical stimulation to stay happy and healthy. A lack of activity or engagement can lead to boredom. Originally, different breeds were bred to have different jobs. Even companion breeds were meant to spend all day with their humans, but these days many dogs spend hours alone while their humans go off to work or to run errands. Doggy boredom can lead to problem behaviors such as chewing, digging, barking, or even separation anxiety. More importantly, it can lead to an unhappy dog.

Example: Your dog has started to chew on your furniture, shoes, or anything they can find. This action may indicate they are bored and need more physical and mental stimulation. (Note: Puppy chewing is a natural part of growing up. Like human babies, puppies explore their world through their mouths. Also, until around eight months, puppies typically have new teeth coming in and chewing helps relieve sore gums.)

Attention Seeking: Just like humans, dogs need a certain amount of mental stimulation in order to be happy and calm. It's normal for a new puppy to jump on you when you get home or whine when you leave them alone, but continuing excessive begging, nudging, whining, barking, and jumping up on you, are all examples of attention seeking behaviors.

Example: You come home tired and ready to relax, but your pup is ready to engage and play or they want continuous petting. Whatever the attention seeking behavior is, you will need to be mindful of how you respond. You may inadvertently reinforce unwanted deeds.

Accidental Encouragement: Somewhere along the way, your furry friend may have inadvertently learned that his or her bad behavior is acceptable. Without meaning to, you may be giving your dog encouragement for misconduct. If he barks when he wants to go outside and you respond, he will learn that barking is an appropriate method of getting your attention. Even if you only on rare occasions give in to those puppy dog eyes and sneak him some scraps, your dog has learned that there is a chance begging will work in his favor. If this is the case, why should he stop?

Example: The doorbell rings, which in many houses prompts the dog to start barking. This barking prompts the pet owner to start yelling, and instead of stopping, he or she just barks more.

Fear or Anxiety: Dogs can experience fear or anxiety for various reasons, including unfamiliar sounds, sights, or smells, past traumatic experiences, or changes in their routine. This can cause problematic acts such as cowering, hiding, barking, biting, or destructive chewing.

Example: Your dog used to be friendly with visitors, but now they bark and growl at them. This could be a sign of fear or anxiety triggered by something that happened during a previous visit. Or, another example is maybe you have decorated your house with decorations for the holidays.

27

Your pup might not understand why there is now a ten-foot-tall Santa sitting in the yard.

Territorial Behavior: Dogs are naturally territorial, and they may bark or growl at strangers, visitors, or other animals as a way of protecting their space. This can become problematic when it becomes excessive or aggressive.

Example: Your dog barks, growls, and if given the opportunity, runs out at the mailman or any delivery person who comes to your door. This may indicate a territorial issue that needs to be addressed.

Lack of Training: Dogs need proper training and socialization to learn acceptable behavior and to communicate effectively with their human family. Lack of training can result in problematic tactics such as jumping, biting, digging, barking, or destroying things.

Example: Your dog jumps on visitors or pulls on their leash when you go for a walk. This may be a result of not enough training or exercise.

Health Issues: Sometimes, troublesome behaviors in dogs can be a sign of underlying health problems. Issues like pain, arthritis, ear infections, or vision problems can cause dogs to act out in ways that are hard to understand.

Examples: If your typically calm dog suddenly starts acting aggressively, he could possibly have a thyroid issue. If your previously housebroken dog starts urinating in the house, he or she could have a urinary tract infection. If your dog has started barking at nothing almost constantly, which is out of character for them, this may be a sign of a serious health problem that needs to be addressed. Pay attention to your dog's symptoms and if there is a sudden change in behavior make an appointment to see the veterinarian.

Bad habits can be very frustrating and sometimes hard to handle, but once you have determined the root cause of your pup's poor conduct, you will be better equipped to eliminate the issues for good.

Chapter Five

A Few Basics:
Housebreaking to Crate Training

Housebreaking

Housebreaking your puppy or adult dog is one of the most important steps in having a happy and well-behaved pet. If done properly, it will help ensure that you and your dog have a harmonious relationship and that your home is kept clean and hygienic.

Housebreaking your canine companion is not an easy process, but it can be done with patience and dedication. By following the tips outlined in this chapter, you should be able to successfully teach your puppy or adult dog to relieve themselves in a location you have designated as acceptable.

Basic Tools

Before you begin training your furry friend, you need to make sure that you have the right supplies. You'll need an appropriately sized dog crate, puppy pads, and treats. If you are housebreaking an adult dog, you may also need a leash and collar.

Set a Schedule

You should set up a regular schedule for potty breaks and walks. For puppies, plan on taking them out every one to two hours. Once every four hours should be adequate for adult dogs.

Start With the Basics

First, you need to teach your puppy or dog where they should go to do their business. If you are using puppy pads, you should place them in a designated area. For adult dogs, you'll want to take them outside to a specific spot and use a command such as, "Go potty," or something similar.

Positive Praise

Once your puppy or dog has gone to the bathroom in the designated area, use positive reinforcement by praising them or giving them a treat. This will help reinforce the behavior you want and make it easier for them to learn.

Establishing a Routine

Once your pup has learned the basics, you can start to establish a routine. This means taking them out at set times throughout the day and taking them out after they eat and drink. Watch out for signs that they need to go. If your puppy or dog is sniffing, circling, or pacing, then those are all signs that they need to go. Do not wait. Otherwise, you may find yourself cleaning up an accident. The more your dog goes in the wrong place, the more this could be reinforced, and of-course you want the opposite results. This is when a doggy door can come in handy if your living arrangement can provide for it.

Cleaning Up Accidents

Accidents are going to happen, so be prepared to clean them up quickly and effectively. Since dogs have a keen sense of smell, use a cleaning product specifically made for this purpose. Have it on hand in easy reach to use for any messes that your furry friend makes. If you can, you should also try to clean up any messes immediately to help them learn that this deed is not acceptable.

Be Patient

Do not show your frustration when your puppy or adult dog has an accident. It will take time for them to learn and understand the rules. Being patient and consistent with a positive attitude will give the best results.

Excited or Submissive Urination

Often, puppies have less bladder control but learn to manage their urination as they mature. If your adult dog is having this issue, have your veterinarian check for any medical reasons for the accidents.

Once you know the problem is not medical in nature, the first step is to identify the cause so you can develop an effective plan of action to remedy the situation. Is it submissiveness or excitement?

Submissive urination could be due to separation anxiety, or fear of the unknown such as meeting a new person or dog. For example, if your pup is displaying improper submissive urination in response to another dog or person, take time to slowly introduce them in order to help them become more comfortable.

Submissive urination is sometimes caused by the lack of early socialization. It can also be due to inappropriate discipline, and harsh treatment. Or it could just mean that your furry companion has a timid or shy disposition. Whatever the reason, training your pup to stop improper submissive urination is an important part of ensuring that they behave appropriately and are comfortable in all environments.

Excited urination is different from submissive urination in that it is not accompanied by fearful body language, such as shaking, averting eye contact, and tail tucking. It occurs more when your dog becomes overly excited through social or playful stimulation.

For example, if you come home after being gone for a while, your dog may become overly excited to see you. Try keeping your greeting low key and distract him or her with a treat. This could reduce the excited peeing over time.

If your pup gets overly excited and pees when a stranger approaches for petting or play, encourage your dog to remain calm with soothing words and a relaxed demeanor. Use a slow and composed approach with the introduction of this new person. You will want to make a point of gradually increasing the number of new people your dog meets over time.

Be patient and understanding when your pup has an accident. It may take some time for him or her to gain more control. If your dog doesn't start to show any improvements, a qualified pet behavior specialist may be helpful in understanding your pup's triggers and what strategies could be employed. Be consistent with potty breaks and reserve vigorous playtime for when you are outside.

Crate Training Your Puppy or Adult Dog

For some families, crate training your puppy or adult dog is an important part of having a happy and well-behaved pet. It can help with potty training, and you will be able to keep your pet safe and secure if you have to be away. Also, it's a place your pup can go when he or she is getting over-stimulated or stressed out.

Contrary to what some people may believe, keeping your dog in a crate is not at all "inhumane" or a form of punishment. When done correctly, crate training is the best way to teach your dog to utilize a calm and safe environment as a tool to help them relax when they need to.

What You'll Need

Before you begin crate training your furry pet, you will want to make sure that you have the right supplies. You'll need a crate, treats, and a blanket or bedding to make the crate comfortable and inviting.

It's important that you get a crate size that fits your puppy or adult dog. It should be big enough for them to move around and stand up in, but not so big that they can use one end as a bathroom and the other end as a bedroom.

First Encounters

When introducing your canine companion to the crate, make it a positive experience. Start by placing treats and toys inside and allow them to explore it on their own. You can also place a blanket or bedding inside to make the crate more inviting. They especially love something with your scent on it. Maybe you have a blanket or a throw that you both share.

Once your pup is comfortable with the crate, you can start to gradually increase the amount of time they spend in it. You can do this by placing treats or toys in the crate and leaving the door open while they explore. Let them move about freely from outside to inside as they please. You can begin to use it as their safe place before closing them in. Encourage them to go in and relax. This may take some time but be patient. It should be a positive experience for your pup.

Establishing a Routine

Once your dog is comfortable with the crate, you can start to establish a routine. This means taking them out of the crate for potty breaks and walks, as well as for playtime and socialization. You should also make sure to stick to a regular schedule for these activities. This will help your pooch learn when it is time to go outside or when it's time for playtime.

Leaving Your Pet in the Crate

At some point, you may need to leave your puppy or adult dog in the crate for a period. This could be while you are at work, or even just for a short time while you run an errand.

When leaving your pet in the crate, make sure they have plenty of water and comfortable bedding to lay on. Check on them regularly to make sure they have regular bathroom breaks and that they're not getting too hot or too cold. Keep in mind their regular potty break schedule.

Crate training your pup can be a great way to keep them safe and secure when you are away. It can also help with potty training and can reduce stress levels for both you and your pet.

Chapter Six

Positive Reinforcement: Building Good Habits Through Consistency

I'm giving this training technique its own chapter because of how important it is to the mental and physical health of your dog and the relationship that you share.

Most veterinarians agree that positive reinforcement training is the most effective method of dog training. It essentially focuses on rewarding your pet for good behavior, rather than punishing for bad behavior.

There are other training methods out there. Some are even cruel and punishment oriented. It doesn't have to be that way. If you train using positive reinforcement, you'll get a trained dog and you will maintain the spirit of that dog.

Here are some tips on how to do this effectively:

1. *Be consistent*: As I said many times already, consistency is important because dogs learn best when they know what to expect This means using the same commands, rewards, and consequences for specific actions every time. For example, if you want to teach your dog to sit, use the same command, "Sit," every time and reward them every time they do it correctly. This goes for everyone in the household who has interactions with the dog.

2. *Use positive rewards*: This can include praise, head rubs, toys, playtime, or treats. Anything your pup finds rewarding. It is important to reward your dog immediately after they perform the desired behavior, as this helps to establish a clear cause-and-effect relationship between the act and the reward.

3. *Be patient*: Training takes time. Every dog is different and will learn at their own pace. Do not expect your dog to learn everything overnight. It's important to keep training sessions short and positive, and gradually increase the difficulty level as your dog progresses.

4. *Use a marker word*: A marker word is a sound or word that you say to mark the exact moment your dog does the desired action, fo

example "Yes" or "Good". This helps your dog to understand exactly what you want them to do. A clicker can be used to signify a positive response to the desired deed. Your pup will learn the sound is a good thing because you will reward them in the same way.

5. *Make it fun*: Make training fun for you and your pup by using games and activities that you both enjoy. This will help to keep him or her engaged and motivated to learn.

6. *Have a positive attitude*: Keep it upbeat! Use a calm and friendly tone of voice when training your pet. Avoid using physical punishment or yelling, as this can damage the trust in your relationship.

Consistently reward your dog for the same behavior every time they do it, but avoid giving them treats randomly. Doing this will only confuse your pet. Your dog needs to know he or she is being rewarded for following the rules.

Remember, you are rewarding your dog for doing something right, not punishing him or her for doing something wrong. It takes time for your dog to learn the desired actions and for them to understand the correlation between their behavior and the reward. One of the most effective punishments you can give your dog is to ignore them. Dogs do not like to be ignored any more than toddlers do.

One thing to consider is your dog may not always respond to the rewards you are using. In this case, you may want to increase the intensity of the reward slowly until your dog responds. Also, your dog may start out responding but then become desensitized to the rewards over time. To address this, switch up the rewards regularly to keep your dog engaged and motivated.

A few more things you can try when your dog doesn't seem interested in training are:

- Try training when there is little or no distraction.
- Train in short intervals to keep your dog wanting more.
- Use a high-value treat like freeze dried liver, cheese, or a meat roll.
- Train when your dog is hungry making your dog more interested in the treats you are offering.
- If your pup seems too tired, train before a walk.

Positive reinforcement training makes it more likely that your dog will repeat the actions you are reinforcing and should be included in all aspects of training. It is a powerful tool that can be used to teach new behaviors and to reinforce existing good ones. This type of training encourages your dog to behave because it's fun and he or she wants to please you.

Once your dog is consistently performing the action you want, you can cut back on giving treats and use more praise. Keep praising your dog throughout his or her lifetime to continue seeing the good behavior. There will be times when you will need to revisit the treats, but you should be able to go back to praise once you have sufficiently reinforced the good habits you desire again.

Your dog does not have an episodic memory. He or she forgets an event within two minutes. They have something called an associative memory, which means they remember events based on associations, and not actual memories.

For example, if you put on your sneakers before taking your dog for a walk, your dog will be excited every time you wear them. If he or she is rewarded positively for performing in a certain way, they will continue to repeat this behavior because they associate the task or good habit with a positive feeling.

Our dogs are happiest when they feel loved, safe, and content. They want to please us when they feel this way. Unconditional love is what they offer us and they deserve to be trained positively, with understanding, petting, and treats.

Chapter Seven

Chewing, Jumping, Barking, Pulling on Leash, Nipping, Growling, Running Away, and More

Here are some of the most common bad habits pet parents find our canine companions picking up.

Chewing – This can be caused by boredom, teething, a lack of exercise, or any other number of reasons. In order to address this habit, identify and understand why your dog is engaging in it and then take steps to address it.

If your dog is chewing due to teething, provide them with appropriate chew toys. These should be made of durable materials and should be replaced regularly.

If your dog is chewing due to boredom, provide them with plenty of exercise and mental stimulation. This can include taking them for walks, playing fetch, or providing them with interactive toys. You can also use a bitter apple spray or other taste deterrents on objects you want them not to chew. Provide positive reinforcement when your dog refrains from chewing. This can include giving them treats or verbal praise. Redirect their attention when they do start to chew.

Jumping – Dogs may jump on people as a form of greeting. It can also be due to excitement, a lack of exercise, or any other number of reasons. In order to address this habit, identify and understand why your dog is engaging in it and then take steps to address it.

If your dog is jumping due to excitement, provide them with plenty of physical and mental stimulation during the day. Daily walks, runs, trips to the dog park, and playing fetch are some examples we have already discussed. These activities go a long way toward solving many bad habits.

A way to address when your dog starts to jump is to turn your back to them and give them the sit command. Reward them when they do sit instead of jumping. You can also give them a 'four on the floor' command, where the dog has all four paws on the ground before receiving attention or rewards.

Barking is common and can be caused by boredom, attention-seeking, fear, frustration, territorial behaviors, or any other number of reasons.

If your dog is barking due to boredom, once again remember to provide them with plenty of play, exercise, and mental stimulation.

If your dog is barking due to attention-seeking, it is because they want your attention for something. Just as you would communicate with another person, your dog is communicating with you.

Your dog might bark in anticipation of fun like going for a ride or a walk. Redirect their attention with a toy or a game when they do start to bark.

You can teach them the 'quiet' command and reward them with treats or praise when they stop barking. Note: Some pet owners teach them to only bark on command, such as the 'speak' command, and then reward them for barking.

If your dog is barking due to fear or territorial behaviors, start by rewarding and praising them when they sit and stay calm. Provide plenty of exercise such as leash walking where more socialization opportunities can occur. Redirect them if they get excited. Take it slow. At no time should you allow your dog near a person or another dog if either dog is acting aggressively.

Leash Walking is a skill all dogs should be trained to do. If your dog has a habit of pulling on the leash, just know this too is common. However, it can be incredibly frustrating to have your pup drag you around the neighborhood.

Steps to curb this include:

1. Choose the Right Leash & Harness - The appropriate leash and harness for your dog can help to minimize any pulling and make your walks a lot easier. A harness that is comfortable will fit properly making leash walking a good experience for you both. Be sure the leash has enough slack and isn't too tight. For larger dogs there are leashes that have multiple hand holds that help prevent the leash from slipping through your hands, especially if your pup decides he's going to catch that pesky squirrel.

2. Start with Short Walks - Begin with short walks and gradually increase the length as your pup becomes more comfortable. Start by walking around the yard or block and then move on to longer walks. Again, take your time. Too much too soon could have a negative effect.

3. Positive Reinforcement - Whenever your pup is walking nicely on the leash, give them lots of praise and treats. This will help to reinforce the act and encourage them to continue walking nicely.

4. Redirect Attention - If your pooch starts to pull, the best way to handle the situation is to redirect their attention. Instead of trying

to pull them back, try to get them to focus their attention on something. Point out anything that could be of interest to them or play a quick game. I bring along a small toy for this purpose. Also, I sometimes pick up a stick and my dog will want it. Many times, he will carry that stick all the way home without pulling on the leash. Some pet owners bring treats to grab their dog's attention when they start to pull.

5. Cue Words - You can say something like, "No pulling" when your pup begins to yank you down the road. This will help to keep their focus on you, and they'll learn to back off when reminded.

6. Stop & Wait - If your pup continues to pull on the leash, you may need to stop and wait until he or she calms down. This will help to teach them that they need to listen to you and that pulling will not get them where they want to go. When they turn to look at you, it means they are once again focused on you, and you can continue your walk.

7. Reverse Direction – When leash walking, you want your pup always focused on you. If he or she begins to pull, say something like, "this way" and change direction getting them to walk beside you, or you can walk backwards making them walk toward you. Remember to praise when your dog stays focused and walks with you without pulling.

8. Heel Command – Dogs may pull on the leash due to lack of training or excitement. Teach them the 'heel' command, and reward them when they walk calmly beside you. Some dogs have

to walk by your side to stay focused on you while others can walk a bit in front. Learn what works best for your dog and stick with it

Digging in the Yard is another habit that can be a real problem. If your dog is digging in the yard, do not despair. This too is a common issue for many dogs. Some were even bred for it, but it's incredibly frustrating to have your pup constantly digging and making a mess. Fortunately, there are steps you can take to help curb this.

1. Provide your furry friend with an appropriate area to dig. Choose a spot in your yard that is away from garden beds, flowerbeds, fences, and other areas you don't want them to dig Once you have chosen an area, fill it with sand, dirt, or mulch so that your pup has something to dig in. Bury toys in the designated digging area to give your pup something to dig for. This can be a great way to encourage them to dig in the right place and keep them entertained.
2. Whenever your pup is in the yard, supervise them. This will help to keep them from digging where they are not supposed to and give you the opportunity to redirect their attention if they start to dig in the wrong area. If your pup is digging under a fence, they could escape and can get lost or hurt.
3. If your pup starts to dig in the wrong area, redirect their attention. Instead of scolding them, distract them with something else. This would be a good time to redirect them to

their appropriate area to dig in. Change the items you bury to keep it interesting.

4. Whenever your pup is digging in the designated area, give them lots of praise and treats. This will help to reinforce the behavior and encourage them to continue digging in the right place.

5. Another tip to keep them away from areas you don't want them to dig would be to drop some of their excrement into that area to deter further digging.

Running Out of the House or Away When Called -It can be dangerous to have your pup run off when you need them to stay put, but fortunately, there are steps you can take to help curb this transgression.

1. The first step is to establish a boundary. Make sure your pup knows where they are allowed to go and what areas they should stay away from. Be sure they understand the boundaries and let them know that they are not allowed to cross them. Tip: Before your pup has a chance to check out his or her new surroundings, fill a spray bottle with one part bleach and three parts water. Liberally spray around the edge of the yard or area where your dog is not allowed to cross. When your pup wanders near the edge, give a firm "No" or "Leave It" command until he or she understands it is a No Crossing Zone. You may have to treat the edges from time to time until your pup has the habit firmly

ingrained. Please know, this will not stop your dog from chasing a squirrel and running out into the street so be sure to use a leash while outside a fenced in area.

2. Teach your pup the 'down' and 'stay' command and reward them when they follow your commands. Your dog should learn to drop the moment he hears "down." Practice both commands together, increasing the time and distance from you your dog is required to stay put.

3. If your dog has a proclivity to run off, it would be wise for safety reasons to use a leash or baby gate to keep your dog from running outside the house, especially if their tendency is to escape.

4. Whenever you are taking your pup outside, use a leash. This will help to keep them close and focused on you. You can use a word or phrase such as "heel" or "stay with me." This will remind them not to stray.

5. Remember to use positive reinforcement for appropriate walking, encouraging them to continue doing this.

6. Dogs may not come when called due to lack of training or distractions. To address this, you can teach them the 'come' command. Praise and reward them when they do. If you do this, they will come every time you call.

Attention Seeking is when your furry friend seems to want your attention every minute of your waking life, (more on this in chapter 15). For example, you just arrived home from work, and you're tired or you still have things that need your attention. Dogs do not understand this and can become confused by the signals you are sending. Some breeds tend to be high energy and need to be played with or loved by you more than others. When you do not give them what they want, they can pick up some irritating habits. Remember to give enough exercise and play throughout the day.

Sometimes your dog may just need to chew on something so have healthy chew treats and toys on hand. Be aware of how your dog is chewing to ensure the treat or toy does not turn into a choking hazard.

Nipping or Growling at People -Dogs may nip at people due to lack of socialization, fear, or from playing too rough. Or maybe, they could be jealous of anyone getting near you. It can be frustrating or even dangerous to have your pup become aggressive with guests in public or in your home.

1. The first step is to make sure your pooch is comfortable. He or she should have plenty of space and are not feeling crowded or threatened. If your pup is feeling anxious or scared, they may be more likely to act aggressively.

2. Are they getting plenty of exercise and mental stimulation? These things will help to keep your dog from getting bored and reduce his or her anxiety. Play games with them and take them on walks to help with socialization and to keep them focused and stimulated.

3. Teach your pup to stop nipping or growling when you tell them to. Give them a command such as "no bite" or "stop" and reward them when they obey. This will help teach them that nipping and growling are not acceptable.

4. Whenever your dog is behaving nicely, use positive reinforcement techniques with them. It does not always need to be a treat. Sometimes a nice scratch behind the ear along with a "good boy," will do the trick.

5. If your pup is young and doesn't understand how hard they are biting, teach them to be gentler with their mouths. Treat them when they play nicely.

6. If your dog starts to act aggressively, instead of scolding them, try redirecting their attention. Playing a quick game can coax them into a lighter mood. Do not allow your pup to get angry enough to bite. A safe place to retreat to might be the best option until he or she calms down enough to try again to be more social.

Grabbing Food from the Table or *Begging* -Grabbing food from the table or counter is a common problem for some pets, especially larger dogs. It can be irritating to have your pup stealing food or begging, and embarrassing if you have guests.

Here is a step-by-step guide to help with this.

1. Make sure your dog stays away from the table or counter. If they are nearby, they will be more likely to try and grab any food within reach. Keep them out of the dining area while you are eating.

2. Have a safe place such as a doggy bed or crate for them to go to during mealtime.

3. Give them a command such as "stay" or "go to your bed" and reward them when they obey. Doing this every time you sit down to eat will help to teach them it's not acceptable to grab food from the table or to beg.

4. Give them lots of praise and treats when they stay away. This will help to reinforce the good deeds and encourage them to continue with their good behavior.

5. If your pup starts to grab food, instead of scolding them, try redirecting their attention to something else. Have a favorite toy in their safe place and remind them to go there.

6. Make sure to keep any food that is left out away from your pup's reach. If your pooch cannot get to the food, they won't be able to steal it.

Being Aggressive Toward Other Dogs

It can be frustrating or even dangerous if your pup becomes aggressive during your walks or visits to the dog park. Even if the behavior is infrequent and mild, no one wants to be on the receiving end of an aggressive dog. Fortunately, there are steps you can take to help curb these transgressions.

1. The first step is to provide them with proper socialization. Make sure they are comfortable around other dogs and people and have

positive experiences with them. Enroll them into group training classes, take them to the dog park, introduce them to other dogs, and have them interact with people and their dogs to help them become more comfortable.

2. Teach your pup to heel when they are around other dogs. Give them a command such as "heel, sit, stay with me, leave it, or relax". Reward them when they obey. This will help to keep them focused on you and remind them to stay calm.

3. Whenever your pup is behaving nicely, give them lots of praise. This will help to reinforce the behavior and encourage them to continue being well-behaved.

4. If your pup starts to act aggressively, the best way to handle the situation is to redirect their attention. Try to distract them with a toy or treat. If that doesn't work, give your dog commands such as "heel, stay with me, or leave it" to get them to focus on you. Remain calm, but assertive. No matter how angry you are, do not shout at them. This will only worsen the aggression.

5. Block their view of the other dog. Stand in front of your dog's face to accomplish this. If they cannot see the other dog, they are more likely to calm down.

6. Hold on to them firmly, but do not jerk the leash as this will only distress them further. Walk on by calmly.

7. Whenever possible, try to avoid situations that may lead to conflict. If you are walking your dog and they start to become

aggressive, the best thing to do is to turn around and walk away. This will help to reduce the chance of a confrontation.

As with any type of training, teaching your dog to become less aggressive towards other dogs will take some time, but perseverance is key. Seek professional help if you don't see any improvement after you've been training for some time. Also, a veterinarian can rule out any underlying health issues that could be affecting your pup's mood.

Chapter Eight

Manage Separation Anxiety and Fear-Related Behaviors

Anxiety is one of the most common conditions in dogs and can be accompanied by serious psychological and physical issues. It is usually brought on by stressors such as separation, a new pet or family member in the home, the loss of a loved one, travel, or just about any change in the environment.

Knowing why can be difficult to determine. What you need to know is its not your fault. It is not because you've over-coddled your dog or that he or she was abused. Separation anxiety can develop in any dog and it's not breed specific.

Anxiety related symptoms include but are not limited to:

- Aggression
- Urinating or defecating in the house
- Drooling
- Panting
- Destructive Behavior
- Depression
- Excessive Barking
- Restlessness
- Repetitive or compulsive behaviors

Some of these symptoms may be the result of occasional anxiety-causing events, but any of these can become recurrent and therefore, result in more serious issues. The most dangerous, of-course, is aggression.

If your pup has a habit of displaying stress or fear-related behaviors, here are some tips and steps you can take to help curb these habits.

1. *Establish a Routine* – Dogs love a good routine and they will be calmer if they have one. Make sure your pet has a regular schedule of meals, walks, and activities that he or she can look forward to. This will help to provide them with much needed structure.
2. *Make sure your pet is getting plenty of exercise* – I can't emphasize this enough. Exercise can help to reduce stress and

make them feel more relaxed. Take them on walks, or play games like fetch with them so they have an opportunity to run and jump. Dogs need to be active with plenty of opportunities to play.

3. *Create a safe space for your pup* -This can be a quiet area of the home that they can retreat to when they are feeling anxious or afraid. Make sure it's comfortable and filled with some of their favorite toys and blankets.

4. *Teach your dog to relax when they start to become anxious* – Dogs are very in tune with how their pet parents are feeling so make sure you are calm so your pup can feel the same. Teach them a command such as "relax" or "calm down" and reward them when they obey. This will help them learn how to relax and stay calm during stressful situations. You can do this with clicker training since the clicker lets you catch the moment of quiet and reward it. Have treats with you or stashed around the house so you can catch and reward your dog for sitting, lying down, resting on his mat, or other calm behaviors.

5. *Use gradual desensitization* - By exposing your dog to the situation or object that causes them anxiety or fear in a controlled environment can help to desensitize the stressful situation. For example, if your dog is afraid of being left alone you can start by leaving them alone for a few minutes at a time and gradually increase the length of time you are away. Make a habit of having your dog go to their safe place and give them a reward just before you walk out the door. This way, your dog will associate you

leaving with something good. It will also help to reinforce the behavior and encourage them to continue being relaxed.

6. *Use positive reinforcement* techniques when attempting to distract your canine companion from stressful situations. Stressful conditions (such as loud noises like thunder or fireworks) can be alleviated by playing a game or teaching them a new skill. Give lots of praise and treats as they focus more on the game or training than the loud noises outside. They will learn the noise is not to be feared and will associate the stress with something good.

7. *Counter-conditioning* is a technique that involves changing your dog's emotional response to a specific situation or object. For example, if your dog is afraid of thunderstorms, you can play a recording of thunder starting at a low volume and increasing it as they learn to stay calm. Give them treats and praise when they stay relaxed. This will help to change their association with thunder from something scary to something positive.

8. *Find a reliable daycare,* pet sitter or walker when you need to be away for an amount of time longer than your dog is comfortable with being alone. Sometimes doing this can make all the difference for your furry friend. Hire someone who loves dogs to let them out for potty breaks, and who will interact with them by playing and taking them on short walks.

9. *Speak to your veterinarian* or a professional pet behaviorist if your dog is experiencing severe signs of stress when left alone.

Things you should *not* do when your furry friend is showing signs of anxiety are:

1. *Do not scold or punish*-They aren't misbehaving when they tear up your closet, they're having a panic attack.
2. *Do not use equipment that might be painful or scary* to your pup. For example, shock or citronella collars will increase your dog's fear.
3. *Do not leave your pet in a crate alone* if they haven't been thoroughly conditioned to love it, or are showing signs of extreme anxiety.
4. *Do not leave your dog alone* for any longer time than for which he or she is comfortable. They will not just get over it. Your dog may become frightened or nervous.

It can be difficult to predict exactly what will make your dog anxious, but if you learn to read their body language, you can take steps to prevent it from becoming a serious issue. If you know what will cause your pup's anxiety, you can avoid those situations or even use them as a positive teachable moment.

Chapter Nine

Dealing with Aggression and Territorial Behaviors: Set Boundaries

Dogs are naturally territorial animals, and sometimes this can lead to aggression and overactive territorial behaviors. If your dog is exhibiting either of these, it's important to address the issue and set boundaries in order to ensure the safety of you, your dog, as well as other people and animals.

This chapter will cover the basics of dealing with aggressive and territorial behaviors, including understanding the root cause, setting boundaries, and providing positive reinforcement.

Understanding the Root Cause

Just like people, dogs have their own personal space and they feel very uncomfortable when a new person or dog enters that space without acceptance. We'll call it their personal bubble. Confident dogs have a small bubble and can tolerate closer contact. Dogs that are more reactive have a larger one, which means they need more space to feel calm.

Pay close attention to where your pup's personal space is so you can tell when their bubble is under threat. His or her body language will give you clues (your dog may lick their lips and tense up. See chapter one for more on body language). It's your job as the pet parent to protect your pup's personal space. With proper training you will help them feel more confident around other people and dogs, essentially decreasing the size of their personal bubble.

Aggression can be caused by a variety of factors, such as guarding territory, resources, or a family member. It could also be due to fear, anxiety, frustration, or an underlying medical condition. Sometimes a lack of early socialization, sexual maturation, inbreeding, or a pack mentality can be the cause. In all these situations, a dog may be pushed too far and can transition quickly from reactive, fearful, guarding behaviors to being aggressive.

Some dogs are naturally reactive, but reactivity is not aggression. However, it can quickly escalate into aggression if not dealt with quickly and properly.

By understanding why your dog is acting aggressive, you can better address the problem and develop an effective plan to resolve the issue.

Setting Boundaries

Once you have identified the root cause of the aggression and territorial behavior, you can begin to set boundaries. Setting boundaries is important in order to ensure the safety of yourself, your dog, and others.

Use positive strategies to desensitize (see below) your dog, develop your pup's impulse control, and encourage him or her to respond to only you. Most importantly, make sure your dog understands that certain actions are not acceptable, and they must respect the boundaries you set.

Start with simple obedience training. Teaching your dog commands such as 'sit, stay, come, and leave it' can help to give you better control and communication in situations where territorial or aggressive behavior might arise. Your pup should go down the moment you say, "down." He or she should stay down when you say, "stay." Teaching them to respond to a 'relax' command can also be useful for soothing an agitated dog. Work with them on this daily. Remember, it will take time. Just be consistent and patient.

Most importantly, your dog should come when you call. No waffling. This is one of the most important skills they can develop. Train them to come to you in all environments, but start the training indoors with little distraction. As your pup progresses, you can branch out. This will help you keep them safe while allowing your pup more freedom throughout his or her daily life.

Positive Reinforcement

In addition to setting boundaries, it's important to provide positive reinforcement when your dog exhibits desirable manners. This will help to reinforce the good conduct and make it less likely that your dog will exhibit aggressive or territorial actions in the future.

Again, provide your dog with plenty of physical and mental exercise to reduce stress and anxiety. Exercise and mental stimulation go a long way toward keeping your dog healthy and happy. It can also help to reduce their territorial or aggressive behavior. Always look for ways to socialize your dog when possible.

Using gradual **desensitization** in a controlled environment is a technique that involves gradually exposing your dog to the situation or object that causes territorial or aggressive behaviors in them. For example if your dog is aggressive towards other dogs, you can start by exposing him or her to other dogs from a distance while restrained on a leash.

Choose a cue phrase such as, "leave it" or "look at me," and begin training your dog while away from other dogs. Once you have your dog's attention, add another command such as, "heel" or "down." Remember to give lots of positive reinforcement when your dog looks at you. You will be teaching your dog to pay attention to you and to ignore other dogs when you need them to.

Start with short walks and keep your distance from other dogs using the verbal cues when a situation arises. Over time, your dog will learn to stay calm when he gets near the other dog by keeping his focus on you.

As your dog gets used to the idea of another dog in the area, you can bring them a little closer together until they can safely smell each other and learn they are safe to do so. Back off if either becomes aggressive and try again when both are calm.

Counter-conditioning is a technique that involves changing your dog's emotional response to a specific situation or object. For example, if your dog is territorial towards other dogs, you can give him treats and praise when he sees other dogs keeping their attention on you so he will remain calm and relaxed. This would be a great technique to use along with desensitization techniques. Do not treat them if they are acting aggressive, only if they are calm and focused on you.

It can be helpful to consult with a professional dog trainer or behaviorist for an expert assessment of your dog's behavior and to develop a customized training plan. They can provide you with additional insights and guidance on how to manage the territorial or aggressive behaviors they observe in your dog.

Chapter Ten

Trouble Shooting: Dealing with Stubborn Behaviors

When your dog has a behavior issue that is proving to be stubborn and difficult to modify, it can be a real source of frustration. You may have tried a variety of methods and approaches, yet the issues still exist.

In this chapter, we will discuss troubleshooting methods for dealing with stubborn behaviors in dogs. Then we will go over the importance of understanding the underlying causes for the misconduct, preventing and managing triggers, developing and executing a plan, and providing reinforcements.

Understanding the Underlying Cause

Dogs often display behaviors to express their emotions and needs. If your dog is exhibiting a stubborn demeanor, it's likely that something is causing them to feel anxious, frustrated, threatened, or they're in pain.

Identifying the underlying cause can help you better understand your dog's misconduct and develop a plan to help them overcome it. Consider factors such as the environment, their daily routine, and any recent changes in their life. Observe them to see if they appear to be in pain. A trip to the veterinarian may also help to rule out a medical issue.

Some common reasons your dog may act stubborn:

Distracted – If you have only been training your pup in a distraction-free zone, your dog will think it's only important to listen to you when there isn't anything more interesting happening. Start small, but begin adding distractions so your dog understands that he or she needs to listen to you no matter what's happening. Some examples include: Guests enter your home, a rabbit runs across the road while you're leash walking, or an interesting smell grabs his or her attention. Once your hound has a good grasp of the 'sit' command, add a small distraction, like having someone come into the room. Add more distractions as your pup learns to focus only on you. Remember to reward with praise and treats.

They Only Know What You Don't Want Them to Do – This happens a lot. If your pup only knows what is not allowed, he or she won't know what to do instead. For example, if you have repeatedly tried to teach your dog not to jump up on people, but haven't told him what to do instead your dog may become confused about what he or she should do. Teach your pup a positive action like to sit or go to a special spot to wait for petting, praise, treats, or a game. Train your dog to go to the special spot when he or she hears someone at the door and reward them for doing it every time and they will do it every time (this is called **Differential Reinforcement of Alternative Behavior** and it will be discussed in more detail in chapter eleven).

Low Motivation – If you are training your pup using his or her regular food or with something with a bland taste, maybe your dog just isn't interested in the reward. Get some special, high-quality treats that only you give them. Most dogs seem to like the freeze-dried meats. You can break them into pea size pieces. Some are more excited by petting and/or verbal praise, a toy, or playing a game. Find out what works best for your furry friend.

Confusion – If more than one person in the household is training your pup and using different commands or methods, your dog is likely confused as to which to follow or how to respond. This should go without saying, but make sure everyone is using the same commands and methods. Consistency is so important when training your pup. For example, if your dog is not allowed on the furniture or to beg for food and one family member allows the dog to sneak into bed with them or slips food to your pup under the table, it only creates confusion. Your dog will not know what to do when another family member doesn't allow these things.

Afraid of You – Punishing your dog for bad or stubborn behaviors will make him or her afraid of you which can cause a lot of even more serious issues. For example, yelling at your dog for peeing in the house can cause submissive urination. Punishing your pup could even lead to aggressive behaviors. Positive reinforcement is much more effective in training your fur baby than making him or her afraid of you.

High Energy – Some dogs who appear to be hyperactive are not getting enough exercise. Try increasing your pup's daily activities. Maybe a walk twice a day instead of just once. A game of fetch or any other games your dog likes. Mental games are good, too. Any activity your furry friend can do to tire enough to settle down and pay attention to you is helpful. Sometimes they just need something to chew on. Have on hand a variety of safe chew treats or toys and allow your pet some chew time. Be sure to monitor them while doing so to ensure against any choking hazards.

Hyperactivity Disorder – If you have tried everything and your pup is getting plenty of exercise, he or she could have a hyperactivity disorder. It is rare so you will want to make sure you've tried everything else, especially enough exercise so that your dog is very tired. If your pup is still bouncing off the walls, there are medications that can help. Speak with your veterinarian about a diagnosis and a possible prescription. If this doesn't help, you may want to contact a professional dog trainer to figure out the best way to communicate with your dog in a productive way to make training him or her more successful.

Developing and Executing a Plan

Start by first identifying the desired action that you want your dog to exhibit. For example, if your dog is exhibiting aggressive behavior, you may want them to stay calm and not bark or lunge when visitors come to your house.

Next, create a plan that includes the steps you need to take to help your dog learn the desired actions. Begin by working with your dog on favorite or familiar commands. Create a positive association with training by rewarding even minor successes. Once your dog understands that training is a good thing, take small steps. This should include positive reinforcement techniques such as clicker training, rewards, and verbal cues. You may also need to implement behavior modification techniques such as desensitization and counterconditioning (see chapter nine and eleven).

By providing positive reinforcement when your dog displays the desired action and gradually increasing the difficulty of the tasks, such as adding distractions, you can help your dog make progress.

Make training a habit. By providing short training sessions throughout the day, you can help your dog understand that the desired behavior is the right one and positively reinforce the progress that they are making.

Chapter Eleven

Training Techniques: From Basic Commands to Advanced Solutions

Establishing a Routine

Dogs thrive on structure and predictability, and having a consistent routine can help them feel more secure and less anxious. This can be as simple as having regular mealtimes, taking them for daily walks, and providing plenty of opportunities for play and exercise. Establishing a routine can help your dog understand what is expected of them and provide them with a sense of security.

On the other hand, being too rigid in your routine can sometimes be counterproductive and lead to anxiety for your pet. For example, if you always feed your dog breakfast at the same time, your pet is going to get antsy if you suddenly decide to sleep in. Instead of building a routine on a specific time, prioritize creating consistency around your dog's training or exercise and where he or she eats their meals. This can help support your pet without making them rigidly dependent on exact timeliness.

Teaching Basic Commands

Once your dog is familiar with a routine, you can begin to teach them basic commands. Teaching your dog commands such as 'sit, down, wait, stay, leave it, and come' can help them understand what is expected, giving them a sense of structure. Also, teaching basic commands can help you manage their actions and reduce the likelihood of them exhibiting stubborn behaviors.

Puppies can begin simple training at around eight weeks. Keep it brief about five to ten minutes at a time. Always end the session on a positive note. If your pup is having trouble learning a new command or trick, end the session by reviewing something he or she already has mastered and give them plenty of praise and a reward for being successful. If he or she gets bored or frustrated, it could be counterproductive to the training, so make it fun.

Once you have introduced and begun training your pup in the basic commands, it's time to address their misdeeds. This can be done through a combination of management and training techniques.

Management techniques involve changing the environment and routine to prevent the misdeeds from occurring. This can include providing more exercise and mental stimulation, keeping them away from triggers, or providing a safe place for them to go when they need a break.

Training techniques involve teaching your dog the correct behavior and rewarding them for doing it. Use positive reinforcement, such as treats or verbal praise when they do something right and a gentle correction such as no or leave it when they do something wrong. My dog knows when he's being corrected when I make a sound like, "aah" or "uh-uh." What's funny is I'll sometimes catch myself using the same sounds when correcting my two-year-old grandson. They both understand what I'm communicating.

There are many different training techniques that can be used to help cure a dog's undesirable habits, from basic commands to advanced solutions.

Here are some examples:

- *Positive reinforcement*: This is a common and effective technique that involves rewarding a dog for their desirable manners. This can include treats, praise, or playtime. Positive reinforcement can be used to teach new behaviors and to reinforce existing good ones.
- *Clicker training*: Clicker training is a form of positive reinforcement that uses a small hand-held device that makes a clicking sound when pressed. The clicker is used to mark the exact

moment a dog performs a desired action, and the dog is then rewarded with a treat or praise. For example, if you are training your dog to sit, you would click at the moment your dog's butt hit the ground. Then you give praise and then the desired treat. However, if your pup gets up after sitting and is treated after the fact, they might not understand the precise reason they're getting the reward. If you can make the behavior happen with the clicker, they will eventually understand that the clicker means they achieved the desired behavior and will be rewarded. Remember, dogs live in the moment so if he or she sits after a command and you get up to give them a treat and they follow, they will not fully understand what they're being rewarded for. The clicker is a great way to mark behaviors quickly, helping your pet learn that they have done what you asked correctly so they'll be more likely to repeat the desired behaviors in the future.

- *Negative punishment*: This technique involves removing a desirable consequence after an undesired action occurs. For example, if a dog jumps on guests, the person stops petting, turns away, and refrains from talking to the dog. Some dog owners use crate training for this purpose. When your dog misbehaves, he is put into "time out" for a short period of time. This must be done right when the act occurs so the dog associates the punishment with the misbehavior.

- *Classical conditioning*: This technique involves creating a positive association between a specific stimulus and a desired behavior. Fo example, if a dog is afraid of thunderstorms or fireworks, classical conditioning can be used to associate the sound of thunder with something positive, such as treats, a game, or praise.

- *Desensitization and counter-conditioning*: **Desensitization** involves gradually introducing your dog to the trigger that is causing the fear and teaching them to stay calm in the presence of it. As your dog becomes less reactive, it is desensitized through exposure to gradually more intense levels of the stimulus. This can be used to help dogs overcome fears or phobias while simultaneously teaching them a new, more desirable way to handle their emotions. **Counter-conditioning** involves associating the trigger with something positive, such as treats or toys, so that the trigger no longer causes the misconduct.

- *Shaping*: This technique involves rewarding a dog for approximations of a desired behavior. You do not teach the final behavior but rather break it down into smaller steps that build toward it. So, if you want to teach your dog to roll over, you could lure them all the way over, or you could shape it by starting with the laying on the ground and gradually adding the next steps to completing the task. For example, if you want to teach a dog to fetch a ball, you could start by rewarding the dog for looking at the ball, then for walking towards the ball, and so on, until the dog is fetching the ball.

These are just examples and the techniques used may vary depending on the dog's reactions and underlying motivations. Be consistent and patient when addressing and stopping discipline issues.

Differential Reinforcement of Alternative Behavior (DRA)

Differential Reinforcement of Alternative Behavior, or DRA, is a powerful and effective training technique that can help you break your dog's poor habits. This technique is based on the idea that you can change your dog's behavior by reinforcing the desired alternative behavior and reducing reinforcement of the undesirable behavior. In other words, you are teaching your dog what you do want them to do instead of what you don't want them to do.

Let's say, for example, that your dog has a habit of barking at visitors when they come to the door. Instead of punishing your dog for barking, you would reinforce them for going to their safe place and staying calm and polite when guests arrive. Over time, your dog will learn that calmly laying down in their safe place is a more rewarding behavior, and they will be less likely to bark in the future.

So, how do you use DRA in your training sessions? Here are the steps you will need to follow:

Identify the undesirable behavior: Start by observing your dog's actions and identifying the bad habit you want to change. It's essential to be specific and clear about what you want to change.

Choose the alternative behavior: Decide what you want your dog to do instead of the bad habit. For example, instead of jumping, you might want your dog to sit or lay down.

Reinforce the alternative behavior: Use positive reinforcement, such as treats, praise, or play, to reinforce the alternative behavior every time your dog performs it. The more you reinforce the alternative behavior, the stronger it will become.

Ignore the bad habit: When your dog performs the bad habit, ignore it and don't reinforce it in any way. This will help reduce the reinforcement of the bad habit and make it less likely to occur in the future.

Be patient and consistent: Changing your dog's behavior takes time and patience, so be consistent with your training sessions and stick to your plan. Over time, your dog will start to prefer the alternative behavior, and their poor conduct will become a thing of the past.

It's important to note that DRA is most effective when used in conjunction with other positive reinforcement techniques, such as clicker training or shaping. By combining DRA with these other techniques, you will be able to provide your dog with a clear understanding of what you want them to do and reinforce the desired behavior more effectively.

Chapter Twelve

Maintaining Good Habits and Creating Lasting Change

Once your canine companion has overcome his or her stubborn behaviors, it's important to maintain good habits to ensure that they remain on the right path.

In this chapter, we will discuss strategies for long-term success when dealing with a dog's undesirable habits. We'll go over the importance of consistency, providing reinforcements, and addressing any issues that may arise.

Consistency

One of the most important aspects of helping your dog to maintain good habits is through consistency. Be consistent in your expectations and the techniques you use to help your dog learn and for his or her overall well-being and health. Dogs thrive with a daily routine. Having structure helps them feel secure and confident because they know what to expect and what is expected of them.

This means using the same commands, rewards, and training techniques every time. It also means being consistent with the schedule for training, exercise, and playtime. The expectations you have for your dog, and the techniques you use will help them understand what you are looking for in a well-behaved pet.

If you have been using positive reinforcement techniques such as clicker training and rewards, it's important to continue to use these techniques. If you want to teach your dog to sit, use the same command, "Sit," every time and reward them when they do it correctly.

Providing Positive Reinforcements

Positive reinforcement is a powerful tool that can be used to teach new behaviors and to reinforce existing good behaviors. It's important to reward your dog immediately after they perform the desired conduct, as this helps to establish a clear cause-and-effect relationship between the action and the reward. It doesn't always have to be a treat. A favorite game or toy or even just a "good boy!" or a head rub and hug can make a huge difference in how your furry friend responds.

Pack Your Patience

Training takes time. Every dog is different and will learn at their own pace. Be patient and do not expect your dog to learn everything right away. Keep training sessions short and positive, and gradually increase the difficulty level as your dog progresses.

Use a marker word

A marker word is a sound or word that you say to mark the exact moment your dog does the desired behavior, for example "Yes" or "Good." This helps your dog to understand exactly what you want them to do.

Make it fun

Make training fun for your dog by using games and activities they enjoy. This will help keep your dog engaged and motivated to learn. Dogs love variety, especially in the treats you give them. Always be on the lookout for a treat they will love.

Be positive

Keep a positive attitude and use a calm and friendly tone of voice when training your dog. Make training an enjoyable time for you both. Avoid using physical punishment or yelling, as this can damage the trust and relationship between you and your dog. Fear is counter-intuitive to positive reinforcement training.

Addressing Issues

Be prepared to address any issues that may arise with your dog's behavior. This includes monitoring their actions, identifying any triggers that may be causing the misdeeds, and taking steps to manage them.

Some tips on how to maintain progress in keeping your dog's good habits in check:

Regular training sessions will help to keep your dog's good habits in check. This can be as simple as reviewing basic commands and practicing them regularly.

Keep an eye on triggers that cause your dog to exhibit misdeeds. This can include things like certain times of the day, certain people, or objects. For example, if your dog barks every time the doorbell rings replace it with a different sound.

Monitoring your dog's progress can help you to identify if there are any areas where you need to work more. If you notice that your dog is displaying the same missteps again, it is important to revisit the training plan and adjust it as needed. This is where a log or a diary can be helpful.

Record when and where your dog is showing good and bad conduct. This will help you to know when you need to step in before things get out of hand and when to reinforce the desirable habits.

Prevent Bad Behaviors by not allowing them to occur. Put shoes away so your puppy doesn't have a chance to starting chewing on them. Pick houseplants up off the floor. Make sure all garbage cans have lids and that toilet seats are left closed.

Remember, every dog is different and what works for one may not work for another. Approach training with patience, consistency, and positive reinforcement. With the right plan, you can help your dog maintain good habits and become a well-behaved companion and member of your household who can participate in family events.

Chapter Thirteen

Understanding Your Dog's Unique Needs

Growth Stages

Training your pup is an important part of ensuring they understand the rules and behave appropriately. Puppies go through several stages of development, and it is important to understand the basics of dog training at each stage in order to ensure your pup learns the necessary skills to live happy and harmoniously in the household.

At 8 to 16 weeks, begin the basics of obedience training. This can include teaching your pup simple commands such as 'sit, stay, come, leave it, and down.' It is also important to begin teaching them basic manners such as not jumping on people and not begging for food.

It's a great time to begin socializing them so they don't become anxious when introduced to a new person or animal. Dogs go through a critical socialization developmental period between the age of roughly three weeks to sixteen weeks. What they learn during that time will imprint on their little brains and have a huge effect on their future behavior.

From 3 to 6 months, continue with the basics of obedience training and socialization. At this stage, begin teaching more advanced commands such as 'heel' and 'fetch.' This is also when you should begin teaching your pup to walk on a leash and to come when called.

From 6 months to 1 year, maintain the training of the basic commands but now you can add more advanced obedience training and socialization. Commands such as 'leave it' and 'go to your safe place' are fine to teach at this stage. Also, continue socializing your pup with other people and animals. This is a key part of ensuring that your dog is comfortable with new environments and people.

Take the time to really get to know your pup and understand what works best for him or her. Remember, training should be fun for you both. If your pup is feeling stressed or overwhelmed, take a break, and try again later. The goal is to create a positive experience that helps your dog learn and understand the rules.

Rewards such as treats and praise can help your pup learn faster and associate positive behaviors with rewards. Note: When using treats as one form of positive reinforcement training, be sure to use healthy, high-quality treats. You only need to give your fur baby a very small amount each time. No larger than a dime. If you are not careful and you give too much, you could inadvertently cause a weight issue for your pup.

By understanding the basics of dog training at each stage of development and using positive reinforcement and consistency, you can ensure that your pup learns the necessary skills and behaviors.

Providing the Right Diet

One of the most important things you can do to help your dog grow up healthy and happy is to provide them with the right diet. Dogs need a balanced diet filled with lean proteins, complex carbohydrates, and essential fatty acids.

Provide your dog with the right number of calories based on their size and activity level. This will help them maintain their health and energy levels, which can reduce the likelihood of them exhibiting any mischief you do not want to see in them.

There are many dogfood companies that provide balanced diets that are essential to your dog's specific breed, age, energy level, and temperament. Speak with your veterinarian to learn what would be best for your pup. Many pet shops offer a wide variety of brands and types from which to choose, such as fresh, frozen, canned, or dried. You may have to try out one or more of what is offered to see which works best for your pup.

I recommend that you change the flavor within the same brand every few months for variety as well as making sure the food you choose is meeting all your furry friend's nutritional needs. One may have more of one ingredient or nutrient than another so you will cover all bases better by cycling through the variety of options offered. Sticking with the same brand will help to not upset your dog's stomach.

When switching to a different flavor (ex. from chicken to fish), start by blending the two together to gradually make the switch. If the brand you are using has dried as well as canned varieties, you can combine the two to give your dog an interesting change. Remember, although dogs like routines (like when feeding occurs), they also like some variation in their diet.

Providing the Right Exercise

Exercise is essential for your dog's physical and mental health and can help them stay active and prevent boredom. It can also help reduce stress and anxiety, which can lessen the likelihood of your dog exhibiting stubborn behaviors.

Some examples are going for morning and/or evening walks, taking trips to the dog park, hiking, swimming, playing games such as fetch or Tug of War, (be careful to set boundaries with this game, see below).

Mental stimulation exercises such as puzzles and treat dispensers could include store bought or homemade interactive games.

---Why Tug of War May Not Be a Good Game for Your Dog---

Tug of war is a classic game that many dog owners enjoy playing with their fur babies. However, as much as it may seem like a harmless and fun way to bond with your dog, it can have some negative consequences.

Aggression: One of the biggest risks associated with playing tug of war with your dog is the potential for it to encourage aggression. Dogs are naturally pack animals, and the act of tugging on an object can trigger their instinct to compete and assert dominance. This can lead to aggressive behavior, such as growling, biting, and jumping, which is not ideal for a well-behaved pet.

Dental Health: Tug of war can also be hard on a dog's teeth and jaws. The repetitive tugging and pulling can cause wear and tear on the teeth and jaw muscles, which can lead to dental problems later in life.

Misinterpreted Commands: Another issue with tug of war is that it can confuse your dog about what is acceptable. For example, if you allow your dog to pull on a rope during a game of tug of war, he or she may start to think that it's okay to pull on your lovely couch throw or even your clothes as you dress or undress. Your pup may also think it's okay to pull on the leash when you're out for a walk. This can make it difficult for you to control him or her and can result in pulling, jumping, or other unwanted actions.

Overstimulation: Some dogs can become overly excited and overstimulated during a game of tug of war. This can lead to excessive barking, jumping, and even destructive behavior, which can be difficult to manage.

---Alternatives to Tug of War Games---

So, what alternatives can you consider instead of tug of war? There are many other games and activities that you can enjoy with your dog that will still allow you to bond and have fun, without the negative consequences. For example:

Fetch: This classic game is a great way to engage your dog physically and mentally. You can play fetch with a ball, frisbee, or any other suitable toy.

Hide and Seek: This game involves hiding treats or toys around the house, yard, or even a sandbox and letting your dog find them. It's a great way to provide mental stimulation and encourage problem-solving skills.

Agility Training: This involves teaching your dog to navigate through a course of obstacles, such as jumps, tunnels, and weave around poles. Agility training helps to improve your dog's physical fitness and coordination, while also providing mental stimulation.

While tug of war may seem like a fun and harmless game, it can have some negative consequences for your dog's behavior and health. If you are looking for ways to bond with your furry friend, consider alternative games and activities that will allow you to have fun without the risks.

Providing the Right Environment

The environment that your dog is in can also influence their conduct. Provide your dog with a safe, secure, and stimulating environment. This can include comfortable bedding, and toys. Ensure that your dog has access to the outdoors where they can run and play that is secure and free of hazards. Also, they should have a safe space to retreat to if they become overwhelmed.

Understanding Your Dog's Temperament and Needs

Before you bring your pup home, do some research about the breed, energy level, adult size, etc. to ensure you will be able to provide a loving, healthy home. Too many dogs are given up because the pet parent failed to adequately do this research.

Knowing the dog breed history and characteristics can help you predict and understand their behavior. Most breeds were developed for a purpose and have innate drives to do specific things and to act in certain ways. In our homes, as pets, dogs still retain some of that drive, and without a proper outlet for high energy behaviors can come out in inappropriate ways.

Chapter Fourteen

Mental Stimulation: Keeping Your Dog Engaged

Mental stimulation is just as important for a happy and healthy puppy or adult dog as physical exercise. Playing games with your canine companion is a great way to keep his or her mind actively engaged. These activities can help prevent boredom and destructive behavior allowing for a more harmonious relationship.

Kids can tell you they are bored every five minutes, but dogs can't use words to express their frustration. Instead, a dog's cry for help usually comes in the form of acting out, like chewing on furniture or barking nonstop.

Mental health and cognitive functions in dogs can also build confidence and release stress. Exposing your dog to unique and novel experiences helps your pup build necessary connections and pathways in their cognitive development.

There is strong evidence that it also will increase the lifespan of your pup. Studies have shown that the combination of sight, scent, and spatial orientation required to solve puzzles and play games help your pooch make connections between different parts of the brain. Dogs are intelligent and want to use their minds to solve problems.

Brain training involves your dog's intellect in a somewhat different way than traditional obedience training, (even though both are regarded as brain training for dogs). Mental stimulation is meant to inspire your dog to think creatively, solve problems, and have fun.

Before you begin any of these activities, make sure that you have the necessary supplies. This includes treats, toys, and a secure space for your puppy or adult dog to play in.

Create an environment that is safe and comfortable for your pet. This means making sure that there are no sharp objects or hazardous materials in the area. If you will be doing this outside, be sure that your pet has access to a place to rest, food, water, and shade.

Start slow with simple games and activities and gradually increase the difficulty as your dog gets more comfortable. If he or she seems anxious, about a new activity, don't force them. You can try again when they are in a more accepting mood. Remember to make it fun.

Interactive Toys

Interactive toys come in many types, shapes, and sizes. They are created for the sole purpose of giving your furry friend a way to utilize his or her brain, and most pet stores carry a wide variety. What's nice about them is they usually have a positive reinforcement component built in.

Interactive toys are a great way for you to allow your dog to engage in learning while you sit back and observe (always monitor your pet while playing with one of these toys or games, especially those with small objects that could be ingested). Most are equipped with varying degrees of difficulty. You can start your pup at a lowest step and as they master it, you can raise the stakes by increasing the learning to a higher level.

Interactive toys come in all shapes and sizes. Below are a few examples.

- food puzzles
- slow feeders
- treat dispensers
- chew toys
- automatic ball launchers
- hide and seek plush toys

Create your own interactive toys with items such as cardboard boxes, paper towel tubes, old tennis balls, rope, old socks, t-shirts, and plastic bottles (always monitor your pet while playing with these homemade games in case an unforeseen hazard develops).

Drill medium sized holes in a short length of PVC pipe. Cap the ends. Add treats and let your pup figure out how to get to them. You can also fill an old muffin tin with moistened treats, then watch your pooch work to get the treats out.

Find the Toy Game

All you need are a few toys and a secure area. Start by hiding the toys in different areas of the room and encouraging your puppy or adult dog to find them. When they find a toy, reward them with a treat and then repeat the process until they have found all the toys. You can teach them to drop the toy into the toy box, giving them an opportunity to complete one of their daily jobs.

Treasure Hunt

All you need are a few treats and a secure space for your hound to search. Start by hiding the treats in different areas of the room and then encourage your pet to find them. It shouldn't take a lot of coaxing.

Trick or Treat Game

Dogs have an incredible sense of smell. Turn over three small bowls and place them on the floor about three feet apart. Have your pup sit patiently by your side while you hide a treat beneath one of the bowls. Teach your dog the "Find It" command. He should stay seated until you say the command.

When you are ready and say the command, he is allowed to smell each bowl and sit next to the correct one. Once he has made his choice, you pick up that bowl to reveal if he found the treat. If he has chosen incorrectly, let him continue to choose until he gets it right and can have the treat.

As he gets better at this, you can add more bowls. Take it slow so that you don't overwhelm him. If three bowls are too much of a challenge, back off to two. Once your pup understands the concept of this game, he will look forward to playing it often.

Kiddie Pool Ball Game

Fill a kiddie pool with balls (no water) and sprinkle treats on top. As your pup walks through the balls to retrieve the rewards, the balls, and therefore the treats, will keep shifting positions. This will keep him or her occupied for a good long time.

Carrot Snatching Game

Cut several holes about an inch in diameter into a flat piece of cardboard. Push a carrot through the hole and when your pet tries to bite it, pull it back. You can start out slow until they get the idea and pretty soon, they'll be able to grab it faster than you can pull it back. When your pup grabs it, let him or her have it as a treat. If your dog doesn't seem interested at first, try adding a little peanut butter to the tip.

Agility Training

Agility training is a great way to give your furry friend mental stimulation and physical exercise at the same time. It's also a helpful way to practice commands learned and a smart first step if you're interested in entering your dog into competitions in the future. Even if you aren't, you'll notice your pup paying more attention to you throughout the day and coming the first time you call. He or she will develop more confidence, especially those shy pups with nervous tendencies.

Agility exercises will also help your dog develop better body awareness such as knowing where each paw is and improving overall balance. Dogs are far more likely to hurt themselves while playing other games like fetch or Frisbee than doing agility training.

Be sure that your pooch understands the basics commands of obedience training such as, "sit, down, come, stay, leave it, heel, and off," before beginning. Start slow by easing into it, especially if training a puppy or a senior. Keep equipment low for pups under a year. Encourage your dog throughout the training with positive reinforcement.

Teaching New Tricks, Games, Commands, and Jobs

Continue teaching your dog new tricks, games, and commands, as well as reviewing those he or she has already learned. Also, give your dog a job to do such as getting the newspaper or putting away toys. Dogs need structure and having a job will help them feel a sense of accomplishment. If you do not give them a job, they'll create one for themselves and you may not like what they decide on. For example, barking at the delivery truck or bringing in special "gifts" from outside.

The key to a happy and healthy dog is regular enrichment with mental stimulation. Also allowing them to engage in their innate behaviors, such as playing, chasing, smelling, chewing, and scavenging. By allowing your dog to engage in these behaviors, you allow them to be physically, emotionally, and mentally satisfied.

Chapter Fifteen

From Ignoring Bad Habits to Developing and Maintaining Progress

Can You Ignore Your Dog's Bad Habits?

You may have heard advice that tells you to ignore bad habits and they will go away. That's only half true. For example, if your dog wants your attention and tries to get it by barking and jumping on you and you just ignore it, you are not letting your pup know what to do instead. What humans consider unwanted behaviors in dogs are usually typical dog behaviors and are inherently rewarding for them. If you even look at your dog when he barks or jumps on you, you've reinforced the action. You have given them what they want. Your attention.

Most of the misconduct I've discussed in this book can't be ignored, but there are some that can be, if done effectively.

Behaviors to Ignore:

- Demand barking
- Jumping up on you
- Pestering such as pawing or nudging with their nose.

Demand Barking –If your pup could talk, what would he say? First, "My human is looking at me!" Second, "My human is talking to me (even if it is, "no")!" Third, "My human threw me my toy!"

You want to make sure you are ignoring the misdeed properly. *Use negative punishment by taking something away.* For example, when your dog barks while you are playing a game with them, you take away the game and you turn your back to them. Or if your pup is demanding something from you such as a treat or a toy, you turn away from them and go into another room, closing the door behind you. Once the barking has stopped you can return and try again. Remember to positively reinforce them for not barking.

Note: You can also use *negative punishment* when your pup is too rough with his or her toys. As soon as you see them tearing into the fabric or shredding the toy with their teeth, take it away and let them watch you as you toss it into the trash can. They catch on real fast and learn not to tear up their toys.

Jumping on You – Jumping on people can be dangerous, especially if you have a big dog and they jump on small children or an elderly adult. Put an end this delinquency right away. What is your dog thinking when he or she jumps on you? First, my human touched me (although it was to forcefully push them down)! Second, my human said something to me (even if it was to say, "off!")!

You will want to ignore this properly. If your pup jumps on you as soon as you walk in the door. Turn around and walk back out. Give it a few minutes and try again until they get the picture. If they jump up on you for attention, turn away. Do not give them the attention they are seeking. Send them to their safe place for a few minutes. Try again once they have calmed down. When they refrain from jumping, give them positive reinforcement with verbal praise and lots of loving rubs. The same goes for if your dog jumps on a guest. Lead your pup away from that person and to their safe place.

Try ignoring any other pestering habits your fur baby might try using to get your attention, but remember to do it properly. Any attention, even if it's negative will reinforce the bad habit.

Extinction Burst – This is when the behavior gets much worse before it gets better. This is why it's important to take care of any poor habits before they become too ingrained. For example, if your pup has learned that barking gets your attention and you suddenly stop responding, he or she will bark more and louder thinking that will solve the problem. Be patient and stick to the plan. It may take some time, but it will eventually be effective.

Supervision

The most important part of ensuring your dog's safety is proper supervision. This means making sure that you are aware of where your dog is always, and that he or she is not in a situation that could be dangerous or put them in harm's way.

If you are unable to constantly monitor your dog, you should consider confining him to a secure area where he can be safe by doggy proofing the area where he or she will be staying while you are away (also see chapter 5 on crate training).

Providing a Secure Environment

Providing a secure environment for your dog is essential to its safety. Always be sure to provide adequate water and a place where your pup can rest and feel secure. Make sure that all potential hazards are removed from the area where your dog is kept, such as poisonous plants, dangerous objects, or anything else that your dog could potentially ingest or cause harm to them. Also, be sure that the area is free of any sharp edges or corners that your dog could injure themself on.

Enforcing Good Behavior

Enforcing good behavior is key to preventing bad habits from developing in your dog and maintaining the progress that you and your dog have made. Make sure that your dog understands the rules and that he or she follows them consistently. If your dog does not follow the rules, make sure to correct him or her and remind them of the desired actions. Be sure to reward your dog for good behavior, and that you gently correct them for performing any transgressions. This will help to reinforce the good deeds and make it less likely that your dog will engage in any unwanted ones.

Socialization

Socialization is an important part of ensuring that your pup is comfortable with people and other animals. Begin socializing your pup as early as possible in order to ensure that they are comfortable in new environments and around new people and animals. Puppies can begin training in socialization classes as early as seven weeks. Veterinarians recommend at least one round of vaccines one week before and at least the first round of deworming.

If you adopted a dog older than four months and may have missed the critical socialization period, of three to sixteen weeks, don't worry. You should still do socialization activities. You will likely just need to be more patient and go more slowly.

When socializing your pup with people, introduce them to as many different people as possible. This will help them become comfortable with people of all types and understand that they are not a threat. Reward your pup for friendly behavior, such as allowing someone to pet them or offering a friendly greeting. Try not to overwhelm your dog with too much too fast. I recommend having your dog sit before allowing someone to pet him or her, (although, some people just start petting without thinking to ask). Having your dog sit reminds them not to jump and to not get overly excited. Be aware of body language that indicates your pup is unsure, scared, or stressed.

When introducing your pup to other dogs, make sure they are in a safe and controlled environment. This can include a puppy class or a dog park. It's also important to make sure your pup is supervised at all times and that they are not overly aggressive or scared.

When you socialize your pet, they are not just meeting a new human or dog. They are being introduced to new smells, floor surfaces, sights, sounds, distractions, and the feeling of being touched by new hands or sniffed by a new dog.

Rewarding your pup for being friendly can help them understand that socializing is a positive experience. Be patient and understanding, as it can take some time for them to become comfortable with new people or animals. Remember that socialization is an ongoing process.

Continue introducing your pup to new people and animals throughout his or her life, and continue rewarding them for their friendly behavior. This will keep them feeling comfortable and confident in new environments and around new people and animals.

It's also important to remember that socialization should be tailored to your pup's individual needs and personality. Take the time to get to know your pup and understand what works best for him or her. This should be a positive experience for you both. It's a time for bonding and teaching. Be patient, consistent, and understanding.

Monitoring Your Dog's Behavior

Once you feel your dog is properly trained, I recommend that you spend five to ten minutes a day working on obedience training. If this isn't possible, train at least three days a week to make a lasting change in his or her behavior. Obedience training includes the basic commands, leash walking, and socialization.

Monitor your dog's behavior in order to ensure that they are not reverting back into any poor habits. Intervene as soon as you see any of them surface. If you catch the misbehavior early, you have a better chance of correcting it quickly.

Chapter Sixteen

Are YOU Ready?

Whose Training Who?

If you haven't figured it out by now, let me just point out that your pup is not the only one in training. You too, must learn new skills to teach him or her properly. Sometimes it's not easy to remember all you must do to make sure your pup understands what's expected. When things get hectic, you might get confused on which command to use.

Teaching your pup hand signals is a great way to improve communication between you. Most pets respond better when an auditory command is paired with a hand signal. Here again, consistency is key. Be sure to use the same signal with a verbal cue each time. Eventually, you'll be able to use the hand signal without the verbal command.

The two most important reasons to use hand signals is first, you can teach your dog to respond at a distance. This is so important, especially in emergency situations like being in danger of running out in front of a car. Second, if your dog cannot hear you, he or she can still respond to the hand signal.

For example, when you use the command, "wait" or "watch me," you can use a signal of pointing to your eye from the side of the face. You can accompany it with, "Sit," and use a hand gesture for this command as well. I use a signal like when the police officer turns his or her palm toward themself and pulls the fingers inward when directing traffic. Be sure to give a reward for completing these tasks.

When you want your hound to stay, put your hand up with palm out in front of you like police officers do when they want cars to stop.

Note: There is a difference between "Wait" and "Stay." Your pup will understand the command, "Wait" to mean to stop and look at you.

"Stay" is often used with the command, "Down" so that your dog understands they are to stay in the down position until released. Make sure you have a command for when you want to release them. Trainers often use the marker word, "Okay."

When you call your dog, point to the floor by your side and teach them to sit in the spot. I point to the floor or ground on my left side since that's the side I expect him to walk on while loose leash walking.

Training Two or More?

Each dog should have an opportunity to learn and adapt to his or her new home and bond with you as an individual. With two, there will always be a competition to get your attention, praise, treats, love, etc. Dogs are social and usually enjoy playing and being together, but what they want most of all is their humans.

Start training them by first separating them so you can focus on each individually. Put one in a different room or in a crate that they have been acclimated to with a furry toy or a chew treat, such a bully bone or a fun chew toy. Their experience should be enjoyable so they do not feel resentful of being locked away.

Keep the training short by taking five or minutes at the most. Then switch the two and repeat with the second dog. Start with the basic commands. It may take longer but what's better than one well trained dog? Two well trained dogs, of-course!

Tips on how to troubleshoot and overcome setbacks:

Identify the problem: This could be due to a lack of progress, a regression in behavior, or a specific issue that you are struggling to change. It's important to be aware of any signs that may indicate that your dog is contending with a poor habit. This can include growling, barking, chewing, jumping, or any other action that is not desired.

Addressing the Issue: Make sure to establish clear rules and boundaries and to enforce them consistently. Provide positive reinforcement when your dog exhibits good behavior and correct any misdeeds.

Review the training plan: Make sure you are using the right techniques, rewards, and commands. It's also important to check if the training sessions are too long or if they are not challenging enough.

Check for consistency: Are you using the same commands, rewards, and training techniques every time? It's important to be consistent with the schedule for training, exercise and playtime.

Look for underlying causes: Sometimes, poor habits can be caused by underlying issues such as medical conditions, pain, stress, a change in the family dynamic, or lack of exercise and mental stimulation. It's important to rule out any underlying causes before addressing the issues.

Working to Prevent Further Setbacks: Make sure to provide your dog with plenty of exercise and attention, as this can help to reduce stress and anxiety. Keep an eye on your dog and to intervene if he or she begins to exhibit any unwanted actions. This will help to ensure that your dog's transgressions do not return.

Remember to make sure everyone in the home is using the same commands and all are requiring your pup to follow the same rules so as not to add confusion about what action or behavior is expected.

Be patient: Training takes time. Setbacks and lack of progress are normal and should be expected. Be patient and persistent, and don't give up on your training efforts.

Emphasize the positive. Reward-based training builds your dog's confidence making for a much happier pet. A happy dog is a focused dog.

Remember, one thing at a time. This means every new behavior you teach your dog should be practiced by itself, not along with any other behavior. Keep it simple for you both, and it will go much more smoothly.

Chapter Seventeen

The Role of Professional Help

Sometimes, no matter how hard you try, you may not be able to cure your dog's wrongdoing on your own. In these cases, it's important to seek professional help in order to ensure that you are training correctly. A professional can help you understand what your dog's training needs are and teach you the steps needed to reach your goals of successfully curing your dog's discipline issues.

This chapter will cover the basics of seeking professional help, including when to seek assistance, what to look for in a professional, and how to ensure the best results.

When to Seek Assistance

The first step to seeking professional help is to determine when it's necessary. If you have been working with your dog for a while but his or her transgressions are persistent with no response to your efforts, it may be time to seek professional assistance.

If you are struggling to manage your dog's misconduct or if you feel that it's a safety issue, then this too is a reasonable time to seek professional help.

What to Look for in a Professional

When seeking professional help, it's important to find a qualified professional who has experience in dealing with dog behavior. Research any potential professionals, check for recognized certifications, and read reviews from past clients

Be sure to ask them about their methods and techniques. Before hiring a professional make sure they are using humane and non-abusive methods that are in line with how you want to train your furry friend.

How to Get the Best Results

Once you have found a qualified professional, ensure that you are taking the necessary steps to get the best results. Be honest and open with your canine behavior specialist, and make sure they understand your goals and expectations.

Provide them with any relevant information, such as your dog's history and health records, so they can better understand your pup. Let them know what you have tried and explain why you think the training has not been effective up to this point.

You may just need a few simple tips or advice, but seeking professional help is smart when you are not finding success on your own.

Final Note

Achieving a Happier, Well-Behaved Dog

The first step to achieving a happier, well-behaved dog is to understand the root causes of his or her misconduct. Bad habits can often be caused by fear, pain, anxiety, or frustration. Or maybe there has been a change in routine, an inconsistent environment, lack of mental and/or physical stimulation. It could also be genetics or that your pup is still in his adolescence period.

By understanding the root causes of your dog's misbehaviors, you can better address the issues and take the necessary steps to cure them.

I cannot say enough about providing positive reinforcement. Reward your dog for good behavior and correct them for any bad conduct. Be sure to provide your dog with plenty of exercise, attention, and playtime in order to help reduce stress and anxiety.

Seek professional help when necessary. If your dog's bad habits are persistent and not responding to your efforts, it may be time to do so. Especially if you are struggling to manage your dog's behavior or if you feel that it's a safety issue.

Remember, every dog is different and what works for one dog may not work for another. Also, know that training takes time and patience. Setbacks and lack of progress are normal and should be expected. It's crucial to have patience and persistence, and not give up on your training efforts.

By following the tips provided in this guide, you can learn how to identify the root cause of unwanted behaviors, implement consistent and positive reinforcement, address common issues such as territorial or aggressive behaviors, and maintain progress in keeping your dog's good habits in effect. You will also be able to troubleshoot and overcome setbacks when your pooch has a lapse in good conduct. We humans sometimes need a refresher course in our own good conduct, too!

Training is not just about correcting poor conduct, it's also about building a strong bond and a deeper understanding of your dog. Training your dog to stop bad habits and acquire good ones is an important part of being a responsible pet owner.

With the right approach and a lot of patience, you can help your dog become a well-behaved and happy companion and family member. You'll have a relationship that will grow where you and your pup can have a happy and healthy life together.

Jessica Broyles has written a practical guide to curbing your dog's bad habits. Through her many hours of training in canine etiquette, she has learned what works and what falls flat. Over her lifetime, she has raised many pups of various breeds. Using positive reinforcement techniques, she has successfully trained her dogs to be happy, healthy companions. Over the years, she also, has bred American Kennel Club registered American Cocker Spaniels, and Rottweilers. Jessica Broyles is a retired high school counselor and lives with her husband and golden doodle, Charlie, in Titusville, FL.

Made in the USA
Columbia, SC
13 March 2024

32589539R00074